Workbook

For

Honest Aging

An Insider's Guide to the Second Half of Life

EvolveMind Publishers

Table Of Contents

How to Use this Workbook

Thank you for choosing this companion workbook for **"Honest Aging: An Insider's Guide to the Second Half of Life"** by Rosanne M. Leipzig. This section will guide you on how to effectively utilize this workbook to enhance your understanding and personal growth.

Familiarize Yourself with the Original Book

Before diving into the workbook, it is recommended to read the original book, **"Honest Aging: An Insider's Guide to the Second Half of Life"** by Rosanne M. Leipzig. This will provide a solid foundation and context for the exercises and self-reflection questions in the workbook.

Start with the Summary of the Original Book

The workbook begins with a summary of the original book. This summary serves as a refresher, highlighting the main concepts and ideas discussed in the original book. Take your time to read and absorb this summary to refresh your knowledge.

Explore the Chapter Summaries

After reviewing the summary, delve into the chapter summaries provided within the workbook. These summaries condense the key points of each chapter from the original book. By revisiting these summaries, you can extract the main ideas and reinforce your understanding.

Engage with the Self-Reflection Questions

The workbook offers self-reflection questions at the end of each chapter. These questions are designed to encourage introspection and deep thinking about the concepts presented in the book. Take the time to reflect on each question and consider your own experiences, beliefs, and perspectives. Write down your responses in a journal or directly in the workbook.

Embrace the Life-Changing Exercises

In addition to the self-reflection questions, the workbook includes specific life-changing exercises. These exercises provide practical activities and prompts for personal growth and development. Engage wholeheartedly with these exercises, as they offer an opportunity for tangible implementation of the book's teachings. Take the time to complete each exercise thoroughly and honestly.

Self-Evaluation Questions

Towards the end of the workbook, you will find a section titled "Self-Evaluation Questions." These questions encourage introspection on your progress and growth during the workbook journey. Reflect on your experiences with the exercises and self-reflection questions. Assess your personal growth, insights gained, and actions taken as a result of working through the workbook.

Create a Personal Action Plan

Based on your self-evaluation and insights gained, it is beneficial to create a personal action plan. Identify specific steps you can take to implement the principles and concepts from the workbook into your daily life. This plan will serve as a roadmap for continued growth and development beyond the workbook.

How to Make the Most of This Workbook

- Approach this workbook as a companion to the original book, using it to reinforce your understanding and deepen your engagement with the material.

- Take your time with the self-reflection questions and exercises. Personal growth is a gradual process, and these activities are meant to be explored thoughtfully.

- Use this workbook as a tool for self-discovery and personal development. You may find new insights and opportunities for growth as you engage with the content.

- Feel free to revisit the workbook and your responses as often as you like. The journey of self-improvement is ongoing, and this resource can be a valuable companion along the way.

Remember, this companion workbook is designed to enhance your reading experience and facilitate personal transformation. Take your time, be open to self-discovery, and embrace the opportunity for growth. Enjoy your journey through **"Honest Aging"** and the companion workbook.

Quick Summary

Rosanne M. Leipzig's book "**Honest Aging: An Insider's Guide to the Second Half of Life"** provides a thorough examination of aging and insightful advice on how to handle the possibilities and problems that come with being older. Leipzig stresses the value of accepting aging as a normal and natural process, dispelling myths, and taking a positive outlook throughout the whole book. The significance of independence, reassessing expectations, and defying ageism are among the major topics.

The book focuses on comprehending the subtleties of regular aging while addressing a variety of age-related topics. To guarantee the greatest potential health results, it addresses the dangers and advantages of pharmaceuticals and highlights the need for individualized therapy and medication reconciliation.

The emphasis is mostly on prevention, and readers are urged to adopt preventative measures to preserve their health and well-being. This includes vaccinations, early disease detection, and modifying lifestyle factors to lower the chance of contracting illnesses. It is emphasized that early screening is an essential tool for intervention and suffering reduction. In addition, the book advocates for the adoption of consistent exercise regimens, dietary monitoring, and stress-reduction techniques as vital elements of a good aging lifestyle.

The differences between dementia and normal aging are examined in terms of cognitive changes and abilities that accompany aging. There are strategies for handling extreme energy depletion and stress management provided to readers to assist them in staying mentally sharp. The significance of mobility, freedom, and safety for senior citizens and their families is emphasized throughout the book.

Studies have shown that sleep cycles are important for general health, with seven to eight hours of sleep each night being necessary for older persons. The book offers insights into the understanding and treatment of urine problems, including incontinence and nocturia, which are connected to age-associated diseases and the weakening of the bladder muscles. Exercises for the pelvic floor and urge suppression are recommended as treatment alternatives, and patients with diseases such as overflow incontinence, functional incontinence, and symptoms of benign prostatic hyperplasia (BPH) are advised to see medical professionals.

As one of the most prevalent signs of aging, pain and discomfort are felt by a large percentage of the elderly population. The book provides a variety of pain treatment techniques, including nonpharmacologic methods like cold and exercise as well as prescription and over-the-counter drugs.

The book encourages readers to adjust and handle these changes with an open mentality by addressing the changes that aging brings about in sexual desire, openness, and bodily perception. It emphasizes how crucial it is to have candid discussions about gender identity and sexual orientation with loved ones, friends, and medical professionals.

"**Honest Aging**" is an insightful and practical guide to aging openly and gracefully. Overall, the book supports the idea that the second half of life may be a time of progress, fulfillment, and continued vitality.

Part I. Aging 101

It's Only Aging, Get a Grip!

Chapter Summary

Rosanne M. Leipzig stresses the value of accepting aging as a normal process in this first chapter. She advises readers to approach the limits and changes that occur with aging with an attitude of flexibility, resilience, and adaptation. Leipzig emphasizes the need to dispel unfavorable aging stereotypes and works to advance good perceptions of strong, independent older people.

She emphasizes the necessity to recognize and embrace the changing reality and reminds us that old age is still a relatively new notion in society. The chapter promotes adopting a "glass half full" mindset and finding comedy in everyday circumstances. A satisfying old age may be attained by adopting a healthy lifestyle, controlling stress and anxiety well, and accepting the obstacles that come with growing older.

Leipzig also exhorts readers to strive for independence, reevaluate their expectations, and oppose ageism. It is recommended that caregivers discuss choices with one another, put open communication above directives, and make sure their viewpoints are taken into account.

Key Takeaways

1. Embrace the changes and limitations that come with aging with resilience and adaptability.

2. Challenge negative stereotypes associated with aging and surround yourself with empowering images of older individuals.

3. Recognize that old age is a relatively recent societal concept and be open to accepting and navigating its unique challenges.

4. Cultivate a positive perspective on later life by finding humor in situations and adopting a "glass half full" mentality.

5. Work towards a happier old age by maintaining a healthy lifestyle, effectively managing stress and anxiety, and confronting the challenges of aging.

Self-Reflection Questions

1. How have you embraced the changes and limitations that aging has brought into your life?

---

2. In what ways have you challenged or confronted negative stereotypes related to aging, and how can you further promote positive images of older individuals?

_____

_____

_____

_____

_____

_____

_____

_____

_____

_____

_____

3. What aspects of old age do you find most challenging, and how can you adjust your perspective to navigate them more effectively?

_____

_____

_____

_____

_____

_____

_____

_____

_____

_____

_____

_____

4. How do you currently approach life's situations with humor, and in what ways can you enhance your ability to find levity in everyday experiences?

_____

5. What steps have you taken to maintain a healthy lifestyle in the context of aging, and how can you further improve your well-being?

_____

_____

_____

_____

6. Are there specific strategies you employ to manage stress and anxiety related to aging, and how can you enhance your coping mechanisms?

_____

_____

_____

_____

_____

_____

_____

_____

_____

_____

_____

7. How can you resist ageism, recalibrate your expectations, and strive for greater independence in your own life or in your role as a caregiver?

_____

_____

Life-Changing Exercises

1. Create a daily journal to document and reflect upon the changes and experiences associated with aging. Write down your thoughts, feelings, and any challenges you encounter.

2. Develop a visual collage or vision board that showcases empowering images of older individuals who have led fulfilling lives. Display it prominently in your living space.

3. Engage in a regular practice of humor and laughter. Seek out activities, media, or social interactions that bring joy and humor into your life.

4. Establish a personalized wellness plan that addresses physical, mental, and emotional health. Include specific goals and action steps to enhance your overall well-being.

5. Organize a family or group discussion about aging, focusing on shared experiences, concerns, and aspirations. Ensure that all voices are heard, and consider possible collaborative solutions for navigating aging-related challenges.

What's Normal Aging? Or, 80 Isn't 60

Chapter Summary

Rosanne M. Leipzig examines the nuances of typical aging and how it varies throughout generations in this second chapter. Our bodies and minds undergo a variety of functional, psychological, and physical changes as we age. Aging is a complicated process. Although these alterations are thought to be typical, how they appear will vary depending on the historical period of a person's birth. Our medical issues, stress reactions, available treatments, and the advantages and disadvantages of each are all impacted by normal aging.

All age groups have physiological changes, which may be understood and addressed to drastically lower the chance of mishaps and avoid negative side effects. Older persons are more susceptible to severe diseases, side effects from drugs, trauma, and harsh weather conditions, all of which may lead to a condition called homeostasis. The safety and effectiveness of novel medicines are mostly determined by clinical studies, however, many drugs are licensed without sufficient research in the elderly.

Leipzig stresses the need to comprehend the fundamental causes of geriatric syndromes as doing so might result in better preventative and therapeutic approaches. She also emphasizes the need for customized treatment, which entails modifying medical recommendations to take into account a person's objectives and life expectancy.

Key Takeaways

1. Normal aging encompasses a range of physical, psychological, and functional changes that vary by generation.

2. Aging has a profound impact on medical conditions, stress responses, and treatment options, necessitating a more tailored approach to healthcare.

3. Physiological changes are a common thread in aging, and addressing them can mitigate accidents and adverse side effects.

4. Older adults are at higher risk for severe illnesses, medication side effects, trauma, and environmental extremes, contributing to homeostenosis.

5. Clinical trials are essential for assessing the safety and benefits of new treatments, highlighting the

need for better representation of older adults in these trials.

Self-Reflection Questions

1. How have you personally witnessed or experienced the effects of normal aging on your physical and mental well-being?

_____

_____

_____

_____

_____

_____

_____

_____

_____

_____

_____

_____

2. In what ways have you adapted your medical or healthcare choices to account for the changes associated with aging?

_____

_____

_____

3. Are there specific physiological changes that you've noticed as you've aged, and how have you managed or addressed them?

_____

_____

_____

_____

_____

_____

_____

_____

_____

_____

_____

_____

4. Consider the vulnerability of older adults to serious illnesses and adverse medication effects. How can you take proactive steps to minimize these risks in your own life or in your care for others?

_____

_____

_____

_____

5. Reflect on your understanding of geriatric syndromes. How can you enhance your knowledge of their underlying causes and potential prevention or treatment strategies?

_____

_____

_____

_____

_____

_____

_____

_____

_____

_____

_____

6. In what areas of your healthcare or lifestyle do you see potential for individualized, age-specific adjustments?

_____

_____

_____

_____

_____

_____

_____

_____

_____

_____

_____

_____

7. How can you ensure that your healthcare and medical decisions align with your life expectancy and personal priorities?

_____

_____

Life-Changing Exercises

1. Maintain a detailed journal of your physical and mental changes as you age. Use this record to reflect on your experiences and share them with your healthcare provider.

2. Conduct research and educate yourself about clinical trials related to conditions or treatments relevant to your age group. Consider participating if you meet the criteria.

3. Evaluate your medication regimen in consultation with your healthcare provider, ensuring that the drugs you take are suitable for your age and health status.

4. Organize a discussion or seminar within your community to raise awareness of the unique challenges associated with aging and to share insights on effective ways to address them.

5. Develop a comprehensive plan for aging that aligns your healthcare and lifestyle with your expected life span and personal values. Share this plan with loved ones and healthcare professionals for their input and support.

Better Living through Chemistry?

Chapter Summary

The important role that drugs play in the aging process is explored in this chapter, along with how they may lead to adverse drug events (ADEs). The differences between older individuals and younger people are highlighted, especially about ADEs' inclination to imitate typical age-related disorders. Crucial to the chapter is the need for honest and open communication with medical professionals, including complete medication disclosure and an emphasis on the higher risk of drug resistance and adverse effects in the elderly.

The chapter presents the American Geriatrics Society's Beers criteria, which serve as a set of recommendations for older persons' pharmaceutical management. These include suggestions for medications to use with care, medications to stay away from, and advice on nutritional supplements. Presenting itself as a practical framework, the Goldilocks Approach highlights how crucial it is to maintain a healthy lifestyle in addition to taking the right drugs at the right times and in the right amounts.

The chapter emphasizes the value of medication reconciliation as a means of ensuring continuous well-being while transferring from hospital or rehabilitation settings. Finally, it offers useful advice on how to sustain a healthy lifestyle, such as keeping a meticulous medication schedule, reviewing it often, adhering to it consistently, and thinking about other therapies when the cost becomes an obstacle.

Key Takeaways

1. Medications play a pivotal role in the aging process but can lead to adverse drug events (ADEs), which may mimic typical age-related conditions.

2. Effective communication with healthcare providers is vital, particularly concerning complete medication disclosure and awareness of the increased risk of drug resistance and side effects among older adults.

3. The Beers criteria from the American Geriatrics Society offer guidelines for managing medications in older individuals, providing insights into drugs to avoid, those to administer with caution, and recommendations regarding dietary supplements.

4. The Goldilocks Approach underscores the importance of taking the right medications at the right dosages, at the right times, and in conjunction with a healthy lifestyle.

5. Medication reconciliation, especially during transitions from hospital or rehabilitation, is a crucial step in ensuring continuity of care.

Self-Reflection Questions

1. How well-informed are you about the medications you are currently taking? Have you had open discussions with your healthcare provider about potential side effects or interactions?

_____

_____

_____

_____

_____

_____

_____

_____

_____

_____

_____

_____

2. Consider the potential for age-related drug resistance and side effects. How can you advocate for your healthcare needs and ensure your medication regimen aligns with your unique circumstances?

_____

3. Have you reviewed the Beers criteria or similar guidelines relevant to your age group? What adjustments could you make to your medication regimen based on this information?

_____

_____

_____

_____

_____

4. Reflect on your approach to taking medications. Are you adhering to the Goldilocks Approach, ensuring that your medications are appropriate, well-dosed, and taken consistently in conjunction with a healthy lifestyle?

_____

_____

_____

5. How do you currently manage the transition between healthcare settings, such as hospitalization or rehabilitation, in terms of your medications and care plan?

_____

_____

_____

_____

_____

_____

_____

_____

_____

_____

Life-Changing Exercises

1. Create and maintain an up-to-date medication list, detailing all the medications you take, their dosages, and any special instructions.

2. Schedule regular reviews of your medication list with your healthcare provider to ensure it aligns with your health status and goals.

3. Implement a consistent medication routine, including setting alarms or reminders to take your medications at the prescribed times.

4. Explore alternative treatment options that may be more cost-effective or better suited to your needs. Discuss these alternatives with your healthcare provider.

5. Initiate discussions within your family or community about medication management, sharing insights and experiences to foster a collective understanding of medication challenges and solutions.

More or Less

What's Right for You When It Comes to Health Care

Chapter Summary

The need to adjust medical treatment to older individuals' specific needs and preferences is the main topic of discussion in this chapter. The chapter emphasizes how important primary care physicians are to the process of jointly selecting the best courses of action and diagnostic procedures for each patient. It emphasizes how important it is to comprehend one's health priorities and objectives since this is the basis for providing medical treatment that is in line with a patient's concept of health. Healthcare may be made more meaningful, less taxing, and useful by customizing it.

The idea of controlling health and finding a balance between the quantity and quality of life is fundamental to the chapter. Setting clear, attainable, and adaptable health objectives is essential to striking this balance. Other requirements include routinely monitoring prescriptions and healthcare activities. It is essential to have frank conversations regarding the benefits and drawbacks of any medical procedure with healthcare professionals.

The chapter gives people advice on how to make sure the healthcare they get doesn't get in the way of their priorities or become too demanding. Establishing mutual respect, promoting clear communication, and developing trust are fundamental values when talking with healthcare professionals about health concerns. To expedite procedures and maximize time for all parties involved, the chapter also suggests concentrating on one or two health objectives before each medical appointment.

Key Takeaways

1. Personalized medical care is fundamental to the well-being of older adults, with primary care providers playing a central role in decision-making.

2. Aligning medical care with personal health priorities and goals is essential, making it more beneficial and less overwhelming.

3. Achieving a balance between the quality and quantity of life requires setting specific, realistic, and adaptable health goals.

4. Regular review of healthcare tasks and medications, as well as open discussions about the advantages and disadvantages of treatments, is critical.

5. It is vital to ensure that the healthcare received aligns with an individual's priorities and is not excessively burdensome.

Self-Reflection Questions

1. What are your current health priorities and goals? How have you communicated these to your healthcare provider?

_____

_____

_____

_____

_____

_____

_____

_____

_____

_____

2. Reflect on the balance between the quality and quantity of life. How can you tailor your health goals to achieve this equilibrium?

_____

_____

_____

_____

_____

_____

_____

_____

_____

_____

_____

_____

3. Do you regularly review your healthcare tasks and medications? How can you improve this process to better meet your unique health needs?

_____

_____

4. Consider your past medical visits. Were you actively involved in discussions about the pros and cons of proposed treatments?

_____

_____

_____

_____

5. How can you ensure that the healthcare you receive remains consistent with your priorities, without becoming overly burdensome?

_____

_____

_____

_____

_____

_____

_____

_____

_____

_____

_____

_____

6. Reflect on your interactions with healthcare providers. How can you enhance trust, clear communication, and mutual respect when discussing your health priorities with them?

_____

7. Are there specific health goals you can set and focus on before your next medical visit to optimize the discussion and outcomes?

_____

_____

_____

_____

_____

Life-Changing Exercises

1. Develop a personal health plan that outlines your priorities, goals, and specific strategies for achieving them. Share this plan with your healthcare provider for collaborative guidance.

2. Create a checklist of key health tasks and medications to review regularly. Establish a schedule for these reviews.

3. Prior to your next medical appointment, identify one or two specific health goals to discuss with your healthcare provider. Prepare questions and insights to guide the conversation.

4. Engage in open and honest discussions with your healthcare provider about the benefits and potential drawbacks of proposed treatments. Seek second opinions if necessary.

5. Organize a meeting or workshop with peers, friends, or family to discuss the chapter's concepts of personalized healthcare and share insights on how to prioritize health goals effectively.

An Ounce of Prevention

Chapter Summary

The crucial role that prevention plays in the lives of older individuals is emphasized in this chapter. It emphasizes that immunizations, early disease diagnosis, and lifestyle changes meant to lower the chance of contracting illnesses are all included in prevention. However, since recommendations change over time, making decisions about preventative actions gets more complex as we become older.

The idea of screening—early identification of medical issues before symptoms appear—is heavily stressed. The goal of screening is to intervene early to reduce suffering and avoid death. The need to incorporate good habits and behaviors into everyday life is emphasized throughout the chapter.

Doing so may greatly improve one's overall lifespan, functional ability, health, and mood.

It presents the concept of an annual health checklist, which functions as a thorough tool for recognizing and addressing a range of health-related issues, such as oral and eye hygiene, primary care, prescription drugs, lifestyle modifications, living situations, and the significance of yearly check-ups with primary care and specialty physicians. The chapter also emphasizes how important vaccinations are in preventing serious infections, even if it acknowledges that additional shots could be required.

Frequent screening for diabetes, which is advised for those between the ages of 35 and 70 every three years, and prediabetes, when treatment is being contemplated, are highlighted as essential elements of preventive healthcare. The identification of diseases in their asymptomatic stage is considered a crucial step in the prevention of diseases.

Key Takeaways

1. Prevention is of paramount importance for older adults, encompassing vaccinations, early disease detection, and lifestyle changes to mitigate health risks.

2. Decision-making regarding preventive measures can be complex in later life, given the evolving nature of preventive recommendations.

3. Screening enables the early identification of health conditions, allowing for interventions to reduce suffering and prevent fatalities.

4. The integration of healthy behaviors and habits into daily life can significantly enhance overall health, functional capacity, mood, and longevity.

5. The use of a yearly health checklist is a practical approach to addressing various aspects of health, including eye and oral care, primary care, medications, lifestyle, living arrangements, and the need for regular visits to healthcare professionals.

Self-Reflection Questions

1. How have you personally prioritized preventive healthcare measures in your life, including vaccinations and screenings?

_____

_____

_____

_____

_____

_____

2. Consider the complexities of preventive decision-making as you age. How have you adapted to evolving recommendations and made informed choices?

_____

3. Reflect on the role of screening in your healthcare routine. Have you actively pursued early detection and intervention for potential health conditions?

_____

_____

_____

_____

_____

_____

_____

_____

_____

_____

_____

4. What healthy behaviors and habits have you successfully integrated into your daily life, and how have they positively impacted your overall well-being?

_____

_____

_____

_____

5. Have you ever created or used a yearly health checklist to monitor and address various health aspects? How could this checklist benefit your healthcare management?

_____

_____

_____

_____

_____

_____

_____

_____

_____

_____

_____

6. Are you up to date with recommended vaccinations, including any necessary boosters? If not, how can you ensure you stay protected?

_____

_____

_____

_____

_____

7. Consider your approach to diabetes screening. How have you balanced the recommended guidelines for regular screening with your unique health circumstances?

_____

_____

_____

_____

_____

_____

_____

_____

_____

_____

_____

Life-Changing Exercises

1. Create a comprehensive yearly health checklist tailored to your unique health needs. Review and update it annually.

2. Establish a clear schedule for diabetes screening based on recommended guidelines and consult with your healthcare provider to ensure it aligns with your health status.

3. Conduct research on the latest vaccination recommendations for older adults and ensure you

are up to date. Discuss any booster shots with your healthcare provider.

4. Organize a group discussion with peers, family, or friends to share insights on preventive healthcare measures and create a support system for one another.

5. Collaborate with your healthcare provider to develop a personalized preventive healthcare plan that aligns with your unique health goals and risk factors. Review and adjust this plan regularly.

Part II. What Really Matters as You Grow Older

Mind Matters

Chapter Summary

This chapter explores the nuances of memory changes and cognitive skills that come with age, with a particular emphasis on differentiating between dementia and normal aging. The focus of this investigation is on cognitive processes, which include memory, learning, attention, language, understanding, and imagery.

The chapter makes clear that dementia is a condition that may cause a severe deterioration in cognitive function rather than something that is a natural part of aging. Remarkably, more than one-third of those who survive into their nineties may develop dementia of some kind.

While aging itself does not cause cognitive abilities to deteriorate, age-related brain changes—such as dopamine reductions and changes in the white matter surrounding the brain's ventricles—can cause cognitive and motor skill reaction times to increase. Adjusting to this "new normal" means using techniques like focused concentration, reducing outside distractions, and creating a calm atmosphere that supports mental health.

The chapter also discusses delirium, a geriatric condition that may result from several environmental or medical factors and often causes cognitive impairment in older persons. The topics discussed include normal pressure hydrocephalus (NPH), which is characterized by a wide-based magnetic gait, cognitive decline, and urine incontinence, and vascular dementia (VD), which is less severe than Alzheimer's disease (AD).

Key Takeaways

1. Cognitive abilities and memory undergo changes as individuals age, with cognitive functions encompassing various aspects of learning, attention, language, comprehension, and visualization.

2. Dementia is not a normal aspect of aging but rather a distinct disease, and a considerable proportion of individuals living into their nineties may experience dementia.

3. Age-related changes in the brain, such as alterations in dopamine levels and modifications in white matter, can lead to increased reaction times for cognitive processing and motor skills.

4. Adapting to cognitive changes involves heightened attention, reduced distractions, and the creation of a peaceful environment.

5. Delirium, a common source of cognitive impairment in older adults, can be triggered by various medical and environmental factors. Vascular dementia (VD) and normal pressure hydrocephalus (NPH) are also explored in the context of cognitive decline.

Self-Reflection Questions

1. How have you observed or experienced changes in your cognitive abilities or memory as you've aged, and what strategies have you employed to adapt to these changes?

_____

_____

2. Reflect on your understanding of dementia and its distinction from normal aging. How can you enhance your knowledge of this subject to better support yourself and others?

_____

_____

_____

_____

_____

_____

_____

_____

_____

_____

3. Consider the impact of age-related changes in brain chemistry and structure on cognitive processing and motor skills. How can you adjust your daily routines to accommodate these changes?

_____

_____

_____

_____

4. Reflect on the strategies for adapting to cognitive changes, including heightened attention and minimizing distractions. How can you use these tactics in your day-to-day activities?

_____

_____

_____

_____

5. Delirium is discussed as a common cause of cognitive impairment. How can you be vigilant about potential triggers for delirium and take steps to prevent or address it?

_____

_____

_____

_____

_____

6. Explore your knowledge of vascular dementia (VD) and normal pressure hydrocephalus (NPH). How can you recognize the signs and support individuals experiencing these conditions?

_____

_____

_____

_____

_____

_____

_____

_____

_____

_____

_____

Life-Changing Exercises

1. Develop a routine of cognitive exercises and activities that challenge your mental faculties. Engage in puzzles, reading, or educational games to keep your mind sharp.

2. Expand your understanding of dementia by reading literature or attending seminars and discussions on the topic. Share this knowledge with friends and family to foster a supportive environment.

3. Adapt your living space to accommodate cognitive changes, such as minimizing clutter and distractions, and optimizing lighting and layout.

4. Create a checklist or set of strategies to enhance cognitive adaptation, including improving focus and attention. Implement these into your daily life.

5. Organize a community or family discussion on cognitive aging and its challenges, encouraging open dialogue and the sharing of experiences and strategies to support cognitive health.

Energy Cycles

Chapter Summary

This chapter explores the idea of "normal" energy levels in aging, acknowledging that these levels may differ throughout individuals and can be modified to account for changes associated with aging. It recognizes that feeling tired is a typical and acceptable reaction to growing older. But the chapter also emphasizes how critical it is to treat severe energy loss as soon as possible since prolonged or ignored weariness may initiate a vicious cycle of weakness.

We talk about the cycle of frailty and how it may be made worse by things like pharmaceutical usage, sickness, physical inactivity, and poor diet. These factors lead to a further deterioration in walking speed, strength, and total exercise capacity. In this chapter, resistance training is shown as a useful strategy for enhancing muscular development and strength as people age.

The chapter emphasizes the need to maintain a regular exercise schedule and keep an eye on one's nutrition to maintain or increase energy levels. It warns vehemently against using anti-aging pills, highlighting the possibility that they won't be able to stop aging or give you back your vigor and energy.

The chapter emphasizes the necessity for thorough examination and consultation with a generalist for help on measures to maintain or increase energy and exercise tolerance, given the possible influence of drugs on energy levels and exercise capacity.

Key Takeaways

1. "Normal" energy levels in aging can vary between individuals and are adaptable to accommodate age-related changes.

2. Fatigue is a typical response to aging, but addressing significant energy loss is vital to avoid a cycle of frailty.

3. Factors such as poor nutrition, inactivity, illnesses, and medication use can exacerbate the cycle of frailty, leading to further declines in strength, walking speed, and exercise ability.

4. Resistance exercise is a valuable means to increase muscle mass and strength as individuals age, contributing to better energy and overall well-being.

5. Maintaining and improving energy levels involves monitoring one's diet and establishing a consistent exercise program, while avoiding the use of anti-aging supplements that may not produce the desired effects.

Self-Reflection Questions

1. How have you personally experienced changes in your energy levels as you've aged, and how have you adapted to these changes?

_____

_____

_____

_____

_____

_____

_____

_____

_____

_____

_____

2. Reflect on your response to fatigue. Have you addressed significant energy loss, or have you noticed signs of a cycle of frailty setting in?

_____

_____

_____

_____

_____

_____

_____

_____

_____

_____

_____

3. Consider the potential impact of nutrition, physical inactivity, illness, and medication use on your energy and exercise capacity. How can you better manage these factors?

_____

4. Have you explored resistance exercise as a means to maintain or increase muscle mass and strength as you age? How can you apply this to your daily schedule?

_____

_____

_____

_____

_____

5. Reflect on your diet and exercise habits. Are there adjustments you can make to monitor your diet more effectively or establish a regular exercise regimen?

_____

_____

_____

_____

_____

_____

_____

_____

_____

_____

_____

6. How do you view anti-aging supplements, and have you considered their potential risks and benefits?

_____

7. Are you aware of how medications you take might affect your energy levels and exercise capacity? Have you sought advice from a healthcare provider to optimize these aspects of your health?

_____

_____

_____

_____

_____

Life-Changing Exercises

1. Develop a personalized exercise plan, including resistance exercises, tailored to your unique needs and age-related changes. If necessary, get advice from a fitness expert.

2. Conduct a comprehensive review of your diet to ensure it supports your energy levels and overall health. Consider consulting with a nutritionist for expert advice.

3. Explore alternative methods for managing fatigue, such as stress reduction techniques and relaxation exercises. Include these routines in your everyday life.

4. Educate yourself about the potential side effects and interactions of any medications you are taking and discuss them with your healthcare provider. Assess whether any adjustments can be made to optimize your energy and exercise tolerance.

5. Organize a group discussion or workshop focused on aging-related changes in energy levels and strategies for maintaining or improving vitality as you age. Share insights and support one another in implementing positive changes.

Ups and Downs

Chapter Summary

The dynamic nature of moods and emotions as they vary with age is examined in this chapter, with an emphasis on how stress affects these changes. Moods are defined as longer-lasting, less powerful sentiments, whilst emotions are defined as strong, fleeting experiences. Stress has been shown to have a major role in the development of anxiety disorders and depression in addition to being a substantial contributor to emotional changes.

The chapter explores the complex functions of the brain and highlights how important it is in determining our emotional and behavioral reactions. It has been shown that some areas of the limbic system and cerebral cortex play a key role in modulating our perception and response to stress and emotions. According to the text, people who suffer from mood problems often show increased activity in certain regions of the brain and decreased activity in others.

The chapter presents stress-reduction strategies including mindfulness-based stress reduction (MBSR) and meditation to lessen the negative effects of stress on emotions and mood. These methods are emphasized because they have the power to alter our brain's physiology and modify how we react to stress.

It has been observed that older persons tend to see life more optimistically and have developed emotional self-control. However, in the first year after losing a loved one, 20% of people may have substantial anxiety or serious depression. It is said that adjusting to this "new normal" is a complex process that calls for both mental and physical training.

Key Takeaways

1. Moods and emotions change as we age, influenced by various factors, with stress playing a prominent role.

2. Emotions are characterized by their intensity and short-term nature, while moods are more sustained and less intense.

3. Stress is a significant contributor to emotional fluctuations, as well as the development of anxiety disorders and depression.

4. The brain, particularly specific regions within the cerebral cortex and limbic system, plays a central role in shaping our emotional and behavioral responses.

5. Stress reduction techniques, such as mindfulness-based stress reduction and meditation,

have the capacity to positively impact the brain and our responses to stress.

Self-Reflection Questions

1. Reflect on your own experiences with changing moods and emotions as you've aged. How have you adapted to these changes?

_____

_____

_____

_____

_____

_____

_____

_____

_____

_____

_____

_____

.2. Consider the role of stress in your life and its potential impact on your emotions and moods. What strategies do you employ to manage stress effectively?

_____

_____

_____

3. How much do you understand about the intricate workings of the brain and its influence on emotional responses? What aspects of this knowledge can you apply to enhance your emotional well-being?

_____

_____

_____

_____

_____

_____

_____

_____

_____

_____

_____

4. Have you ever explored stress reduction techniques such as mindfulness-based stress reduction or meditation? How might these techniques benefit your responses to stress and emotions?

_____

_____

_____

5. Reflect on the tendency of older adults to adopt a more positive perspective on life. How have you cultivated a positive outlook and emotional control in your own life?

_____

_____

_____

_____

_____

_____

_____

_____

_____

_____

_____

6. Have you or someone you know experienced major depression or significant anxiety following a significant loss? How did you or they adapt to the "new normal" in this situation?

_____

_____

_____

_____

_____

_____

_____

_____

_____

_____

_____

Life-Changing Exercises

1. Integrate stress reduction techniques such as mindfulness-based stress reduction or meditation into your daily routine. Begin with brief meetings and progressively lengthen them.

2. Invest time in understanding the brain's role in emotional responses and consider how this knowledge can inform your approach to managing emotions.

3. Create a personal toolbox of strategies for managing stress, incorporating techniques that resonate with you. Regularly apply these strategies to enhance emotional well-being.

4. Engage in open conversations with older adults who have developed a positive perspective on life and emotional control. Learn from their experiences and insights.

5. Organize or participate in support groups or workshops focused on adapting to major life changes and loss. Share your own experiences and listen to the stories and strategies of others.

Balancing Acts

Chapter Summary

This chapter emphasizes the importance of mobility, independence, and safety for older individuals and their families. It highlights the need for balancing management to ensure survival and a decent standard of living. Assistive equipment like canes and walkers can help sustain strength and endurance, leading to improved mobility and safety. Postural hypotension is a common issue in elderly individuals, particularly in nursing homes.

Fall risk factors are a major concern, and addressing fall risk factor adaptation measures is crucial for reducing mobility impairment. The chapter also discusses healthcare coverage, highlighting that physical therapy is covered by Medicare for moderate to severe mobility impairments. Osteoporosis prevention is also discussed, with strategies like joint replacement surgery, rehabilitation, pain treatment, and postprandial hypotension control.

The chapter also covers common disorders like back pain, neurological ailments, dizziness, and drug side effects that can exacerbate balance and movement problems. Physical therapy is a useful strategy for increasing mobility and lowering the risk of cardiovascular disease.

Key Takeaways

1. Mobility, independence, and safety are of utmost importance for older adults, influencing both quality of life and survival.

2. Assistive devices like canes and walkers are beneficial for maintaining strength and endurance, thereby enhancing mobility.

3. Postural hypotension is more prevalent among older adults and can significantly impact their well-being, especially in nursing home settings.

4. Falling is a common risk factor for injuries and decreased mobility, and adapting to fall risk factors can minimize mobility impairment.

5. Medicare provides coverage for physical therapy for those facing moderate to severe mobility limitations. Preventing osteoporosis is vital for reducing fall-related injuries.

Self-Reflection Questions

1. How do you currently prioritize mobility, independence, and safety in your daily life and routines, or in your care for older loved ones?

_____

_____

2. Have you explored the use of assistive devices like canes or walkers to enhance mobility and independence? How has this impacted your or your loved one's life?

_____

_____

_____

_____

_____

_____

_____

_____

_____

_____

_____

3. Consider the concept of postural hypotension. Have you experienced or observed this condition in older adults, and how has it affected their overall well-being?

_____

_____

_____

_____

_____

_____

_____

_____

_____

_____

_____

_____

4. Falling is a major concern. How have you adapted
to or helped loved ones adapt to fall risk factors to
reduce the risk of injury and mobility impairment?

_____

_____

5. Are you aware of the healthcare coverage provided by Medicare for physical therapy in cases of moderate to severe mobility limitations?

_____

_____

_____

_____

_____

_____

_____

_____

_____

_____

_____

6. Reflect on osteoporosis prevention as a means of reducing fall-related injuries. What steps have you taken to address this concern for yourself or others?

_____

_____

_____

_____

_____

7. Consider common conditions that worsen balance and mobility. How have these conditions influenced you or your loved ones, and what strategies have you employed to manage them?

_____

_____

_____

_____

_____

_____

_____

_____

_____

_____

_____

Life-Changing Exercises

1. Collaborate with a healthcare provider or physical therapist to develop a personalized mobility and fall prevention plan that suits your unique needs and goals.

2. Create a safe living environment by identifying and addressing fall risk factors, such as slippery floors or poor lighting. Share these insights with older loved ones as well.

3. Initiate conversations with older adults about their mobility, balance, and safety concerns. Encourage them to seek professional advice or participate in balance-improving activities.

4. Organize a community workshop or information session on fall prevention strategies and promote awareness of the importance of balance and mobility among older individuals.

5. Prioritize regular physical therapy sessions to enhance mobility, maintain balance, and reduce the risk of cardiovascular disease, consulting with a healthcare provider to determine the most suitable approach.

Sleep Cycles

Chapter Summary

Sleep cycles, a fundamental aspect of overall health, occupy a substantial portion of our lives, with approximately a third of our time spent in slumber. Inadequate sleep can lead to a range of adverse outcomes, including fatigue, impaired cognitive function, an elevated risk of falls, and the exacerbation of chronic medical conditions. As we age, our sleep requirements evolve, with older adults typically requiring seven to eight hours of sleep per night.

The regulation of sleepiness and wakefulness over a 24-hour period is governed by the circadian rhythm, which plays a pivotal role in orchestrating our sleep patterns. The chapter outlines the various stages of sleep, with Stage N1 representing the lightest sleep, Stage N2 indicating a slightly deeper sleep, and Stage N3 representing the deepest sleep stage. Notably, older adults often spend more time awake during sleep, a measure known as sleep efficiency, and are inclined to go to bed and wake up earlier due to shifts in their circadian rhythm.

The chapter emphasizes the importance of addressing sleep-related conditions and fostering healthy sleep routines to enhance both the quality and duration of sleep. It also introduces nonpharmacologic treatments for insomnia, such as cognitive behavioral therapy for insomnia (CBT-I). Understanding and managing sleep disorders is identified as a key element in preserving good health and a high quality of life.

Key Takeaways

1. Sleep cycles are integral to overall health, and poor sleep quality can lead to various negative consequences.

2. The sleep needs of older adults typically range from seven to eight hours of sleep per night.

3. Circadian rhythm plays a central role in regulating sleep-wake cycles over a 24-hour period.

4. Sleep encompasses different stages, including light and deep sleep, and older adults may experience changes in sleep efficiency and circadian rhythm.

5. Managing sleep disorders and adopting healthy sleep routines can substantially improve sleep quality and duration.

Self-Reflection Questions

1. How well do you currently understand the importance of sleep in your overall health and well-being?

2. Have you observed any changes in your sleep patterns as you've aged? How have these developments affected you in day-to-day life?

_____

_____

_____

_____

_____

_____

_____

_____

_____

_____

_____

3. What strategies have you employed to maintain or improve your sleep efficiency and overall sleep quality?

_____

_____

_____

_____

_____

_____

_____

_____

_____

_____

_____

_____

4. Are you aware of any specific sleep disorders that may be impacting your sleep? How have you addressed or managed them?

_____

5. How do you feel about the idea of nonpharmacologic treatments like cognitive behavioral therapy for insomnia? Are you open to exploring these options?

_____

_____

_____

_____

_____

_____

_____

_____

_____

_____

_____

6. Reflect on your circadian rhythm and its influence on your sleep-wake cycles. How have you adapted to any changes in this rhythm over time?

_____

_____

_____

_____

7. What steps can you take to better understand and address your sleep-related conditions to improve your health and quality of life?

_____

_____

_____

_____

_____

_____

_____

_____

_____

_____

Life-Changing Exercises

1. Establish a consistent sleep routine that aligns with your circadian rhythm, incorporating habits that promote better sleep hygiene.

2. Keep a sleep journal to track your sleep patterns, sleep efficiency, and any related conditions or factors affecting your sleep.

3. Explore nonpharmacologic treatments for insomnia, such as cognitive behavioral therapy for

insomnia (CBT-I), and consider seeking guidance from a sleep specialist.

4. Organize a discussion or workshop on sleep health with friends or family, sharing insights and strategies for achieving restorative sleep.

5. Collaborate with a healthcare provider to assess and address any sleep disorders or conditions that may be impacting your sleep quality, and develop a tailored plan for improvement.

Urine Trouble

Chapter Summary

This chapter explores the urinary issues that can surface with aging. Often occurring problems include nocturia and incontinence, which are caused by weakening of the bladder muscles and age-related illnesses. These issues may show up as decreased hand and finger dexterity, a rise in overnight urine, and a slowdown in walking speed. Benign prostatic hyperplasia (BPH) in elderly men with enlarged prostates causes increased midnight urination as well as increased urine volume.

The chapter stresses that changing one's lifestyle might help manage these urinary problems, but it also warns against severely limiting one's consumption of liquids since this may have unforeseen health repercussions. Readjusting to a new normal, treating constipation, increasing mobility with assistive equipment and physical therapy, and reviewing medications are all part of managing urinary difficulties. Exercises for the pelvic floor and urge suppression are two behavioral therapies that may be used to treat incontinence, a unique geriatric condition. The best way to handle issues such as overflow incontinence, functional incontinence, and symptoms of BPH is to have a medical specialist evaluate you.

The chapter ends with advice on helping loved ones who are experiencing incontinence, acknowledging that these difficulties may have a substantial impact on a person's feeling of dignity and self-worth.

Key Takeaways

1. As individuals age, urinary issues, including incontinence and nocturia, become more prevalent due to factors like weakened bladder muscles and age-related conditions.

2. These concerns can lead to increased nighttime urination, reduced mobility, and diminished hand dexterity.

3. Benign prostatic hyperplasia (BPH) in older men can contribute to more frequent nighttime urination and greater urine volume.

4. Lifestyle adjustments can help manage urinary problems, but it's crucial to avoid excessive liquid intake restriction, as this can have unintended consequences.

5. Addressing urinary challenges involves adapting to a new normal, managing constipation, enhancing mobility through physical therapy and aids, and reviewing medications. Behavioral treatments can be effective for incontinence, and medical evaluation is recommended for other related conditions.

Self-Reflection Questions

1. How have you observed or experienced urinary issues related to aging, and how have they impacted your daily life and well-being?

_____

_____

_____

_____

_____

_____

_____

_____

_____

_____

2. Consider any lifestyle adjustments you've made to manage urinary challenges. Have these changes been effective, or have you encountered unintended consequences?

_____

_____

_____

_____

3. Reflect on the concept of adapting to a "new normal." How have you navigated changes related to urinary issues and incorporated them into your daily routine?

_____

_____

_____

_____

_____

_____

_____

_____

_____

_____

_____

4. Have you taken steps to address constipation and improve mobility as recommended in the chapter? What strategies have been most beneficial for you?

_____

_____

_____

_____

_____

_____

_____

_____

_____

_____

_____

5. If you've faced incontinence, have you explored behavioral interventions like pelvic floor exercises and urge suppression techniques? How have these interventions worked for you?

_____

6. How comfortable are you discussing urinary issues with a medical provider, and have you sought their evaluation and guidance as needed?

_____

_____

_____

_____

_____

_____

_____

_____

_____

_____

_____

_____

7. Consider how you would support a loved one dealing with urinary challenges, keeping in mind the importance of preserving their dignity and self-esteem.

_____

_____

_____

Life-Changing Exercises

1. Create a personalized plan for managing urinary issues that incorporates the recommendations discussed in the chapter. Review this strategy often and make any necessary adjustments.

2. Explore behavioral interventions for incontinence, such as pelvic floor exercises and urge suppression techniques. Implement a routine and track progress.

3. If you or a loved one are experiencing urinary issues, schedule a consultation with a healthcare provider to evaluate the situation and seek professional guidance.

4. Organize a support group or discussion with friends, family, or peers who may be facing similar urinary challenges, providing a platform for sharing insights and strategies.

5. Initiate open and empathetic conversations with loved ones who may be dealing with incontinence, ensuring they feel heard, respected, and supported in maintaining their sense of dignity and self-worth.

All Eyes and Ears

Chapter Summary

This chapter emphasizes the indispensable role of our senses in various cognitive functions, including memory, spatial perception, and balance. As we age, our sensory capabilities, specifically vision and hearing, undergo notable changes. Age-related visual alterations manifest as difficulties such as blurry print, increased light requirements, and decreased perception of color and contrast.

Remedies for these issues include glasses, cataract surgery, artificial tears, and enhanced lighting. Vision impairments associated with aging can lead to sensations of stinging, burning, or blurred vision. Early diagnosis and treatment are imperative for numerous eye conditions, such as cataracts, glaucoma, and acute closed-angle glaucoma. Treatment options encompass medications to prevent the formation and leakage of new blood vessels, as well as laser therapies.

Hearing loss is another prevalent age-related issue, affecting approximately one-quarter of individuals over 65 and nearly half of those over 80, with presbycusis being the most common form. Adjusting to this "new normal" involves lifestyle modifications, including smoking cessation, adopting a healthy diet, engaging in regular exercise, and exploring technology to enhance hearing. While hearing aids are essential for improving hearing and speech comprehension, they can be expensive and are not typically covered by Medicare. However, the chapter notes that over-the-counter options are becoming more affordable, and emphasizes the pivotal role of family support in ensuring the continued use of vision rehabilitation devices.

Key Takeaways

1. Aging brings about changes in sensory functions, particularly vision and hearing, which have a significant impact on various cognitive abilities.

2. Vision issues that accompany aging include difficulties with reading, increased need for light, and reduced color and contrast perception, with treatment options available to address these challenges.

3. Age-related vision impairments can lead to discomforting sensations such as stinging, burning, or blurred vision.

4. Timely diagnosis and intervention are vital for various eye conditions, including cataracts, glaucoma, and acute closed-angle glaucoma, with treatment strategies encompassing medications and laser therapies.

5. Hearing loss, notably presbycusis, is a common age-related issue. Adjusting to this change involves making healthy lifestyle choices, exploring technology to enhance hearing, and considering hearing aids.

Self-Reflection Questions

1. How have age-related changes in vision and hearing impacted your daily life and overall well-being?

_____

_____

_____

_____

_____

_____

_____

_____

_____

_____

_____

_____

2. Reflect on your adaptation to vision changes, including the use of glasses, enhanced lighting, and other remedies. How have these strategies improved your visual comfort?

_____

3. Have you experienced any symptoms of age-related vision impairments, such as stinging, burning, or blurred vision? How have you sought diagnosis and treatment?

_____

_____

_____

_____

_____

_____

_____

_____

_____

_____

_____

4. Consider your awareness of common eye conditions like cataracts and glaucoma. How can you ensure early diagnosis and appropriate treatment for these conditions?

_____

_____

_____

_____

5. Reflect on any hearing loss you or your loved ones may have encountered. What lifestyle modifications have you considered to adapt to this "new normal"?

_____

_____

_____

_____

_____

_____

_____

6. How can you explore technological solutions to enhance your hearing, and have you considered the use of hearing aids or over-the-counter options?

7. Recognizing that family support is vital, how can you involve your loved ones in your journey to manage vision and hearing changes and continue using assistive devices?

_____

_____

_____

_____

_____

_____

_____

_____

_____

_____

Life-Changing Exercises

1. Create a personalized plan for addressing vision changes and hearing loss, incorporating the recommended treatments and strategies. Review this strategy often and make any necessary adjustments.

2. Schedule regular eye and hearing check-ups with healthcare professionals to monitor and address any age-related issues as early as possible.

3. Explore over-the-counter hearing aid options and seek guidance from hearing specialists to make informed choices.

4. Organize discussions or workshops on vision and hearing health with friends, family, or peers, sharing insights and solutions for managing these challenges.

5. Engage your loved ones in conversations about your vision and hearing challenges, and encourage their active support in using assistive devices and making lifestyle adjustments.

Aches and Pains

Chapter Summary

Pain and discomfort are commonplace symptoms as we age, with a significant portion of older adults experiencing pain lasting for at least a year, and over 15% reporting daily pain. Pain is classified into three primary categories: nociceptive, neuropathic, and inflammatory, with many individuals experiencing pain resulting from multiple causes. Among these, the musculoskeletal system, including joints, the spine, and related tissues, accounts for a substantial 70% of pain experienced by older adults. Osteoarthritis (OA) is a prevalent condition that affects the joints, and it's important to note that sensitivity to pain medications tends to increase with age.

Pain management strategies encompass both prescription and non-prescription options.

Non-prescription medications like acetaminophen and non-steroidal anti-inflammatory drugs (NSAIDs) can provide rapid relief, but oral NSAIDs may carry significant adverse effects. Nonpharmacologic methods, including the application of ice and exercise, are also valuable tools for addressing pain. The choice of treatment depends on the nature and severity of the pain.

Inflammatory disorders that older adults may face include conditions like polymyalgia rheumatica, giant cell arteritis, rheumatoid arthritis, gout, hip osteoarthritis, nerve pain, and fibromyalgia.

Key Takeaways

1. Pain and discomfort are common experiences in aging, with a significant proportion of older adults facing persistent or daily pain.

2. Pain can be categorized into three main types: nociceptive, neuropathic, and inflammatory, with

many individuals experiencing pain caused by a combination of factors.

3. Musculoskeletal issues, such as joint and spine problems, are responsible for a substantial portion of pain in older adults.

4. Osteoarthritis (OA) is a frequently encountered condition affecting the joints, and it's essential to consider age-related changes in pain sensitivity when selecting pain medications.

5. Pain management approaches involve a range of treatments, both pharmacologic and nonpharmacologic, with the choice of treatment depending on the nature and severity of the pain.

Self-Reflection Questions

1. How has pain or discomfort impacted your life as you've aged, and what strategies have you employed to address it?

_____

_____

_____

_____

_____

_____

2. Reflect on your understanding of different types of pain, such as nociceptive, neuropathic, and inflammatory. How have these distinctions informed your approach to pain management?

_____

_____

3. Consider the source of your pain. Is it primarily musculoskeletal, as is common in older adults, or is it linked to other factors?

_____

_____

_____

_____

_____

_____

_____

_____

_____

_____

_____

4. Have you encountered osteoarthritis (OA) or similar joint-related pain? How have you approached managing the pain associated with these conditions?

_____

_____

_____

_____

5. Reflect on your experience with pain medications, both prescription and over-the-counter. How have you adapted your choices to accommodate age-related changes in sensitivity?

_____

_____

_____

_____

_____

6. How comfortable are you with nonpharmacologic pain management approaches, such as using ice and incorporating exercise? What benefits have you observed?

_____

_____

_____

7. Have you or your loved ones faced inflammatory disorders mentioned in the chapter? How have you navigated these conditions and sought appropriate treatment?

_____

_____

_____

_____

_____

_____

_____

_____

_____

_____

_____

Life-Changing Exercises

1. Create a pain management plan that addresses your specific pain type, incorporating both pharmacologic and nonpharmacologic options. Regularly review and adjust this plan as needed.

2. Explore nonpharmacologic pain relief methods, such as exercise and ice application. Develop a routine and track their impact on your pain management.

3. Consult with a healthcare provider to discuss pain medications, ensuring they align with your needs and age-related changes in sensitivity.

4. Organize a discussion or workshop with peers, friends, or family to share insights and strategies for pain management, providing a supportive network for one another.

5. Collaborate with a healthcare provider to address inflammatory disorders or chronic pain conditions and develop a personalized plan for managing them, considering both pharmacologic and nonpharmacologic interventions.

Gut Feelings

Chapter Summary

The aging process often causes pain and even shame in the gastrointestinal (GI) system, a body system that usually functions automatically. Rather than being directly related to aging, GI issues are often misdiagnosed as the result of underlying illnesses, pharmaceutical side effects, or behavioral changes. Important gut-related issues include nutrition and weight control, highlighting the need to modify one's lifestyle, medicines, and activities to meet changing requirements as one age.

Common problems that older persons have are not only related to being older, such as dry mouth and constipation. The chapter emphasizes the function of saliva in the swallowing process and describes the complex mechanisms that break down food into necessary building blocks inside the stomach, including both mechanical and chemical changes. Additionally covered is gastroesophageal reflux disease (GERD), with a focus on how important it is to identify and treat it early to avoid more serious esophageal issues or anemia.

As people age, gallstones grow more common, often as a result of the gallbladder's higher cholesterol content. The chapter makes it clear that while constipation may increase in frequency as one ages, alterations in the large intestine that occur with aging are not the primary cause of the condition. The shift to this "new normal" in gut health calls for certain behaviors, such as taking pills with water and staying upright to avoid pill esophagitis.

Key Takeaways

1. Aging can lead to discomfort and potential embarrassment related to the gastrointestinal (GI) system, which tends to function automatically.

2. Symptoms of GI disorders in older adults are often linked to underlying diseases, medications, or behavioral changes, rather than the aging process itself.

3. Concerns surrounding the gut involve issues like weight management and nutrition, necessitating adaptations in diet, medications, and daily activities.

4. While constipation and dry mouth are common concerns among older adults, they are not exclusively due to the aging process.

5. The digestive process involves complex mechanical and chemical transformations of food into essential building blocks, with saliva playing a crucial role in the act of swallowing. Gastroesophageal reflux disease (GERD) should be promptly recognized and managed.

Self-Reflection Questions

1. How have you experienced changes in your gastrointestinal health as you've aged, and what strategies have you employed to address these issues?

_____

_____

_____

_____

_____

_____

_____

_____

_____

_____

_____

2. Consider your awareness of the factors that contribute to common gut-related concerns in older adults, such as constipation and dry mouth. How has this understanding informed your approach to managing these issues?

_____

_____

_____

3. Reflect on the complex process of food digestion in the gut. How has your awareness of this process influenced your dietary choices and eating habits?

_____

_____

_____

_____

4. Have you encountered or been diagnosed with gastroesophageal reflux disease (GERD)? How have you approached its management to prevent complications?

_____

_____

_____

_____

_____

_____

_____

_____

_____

_____

_____

5. How familiar are you with gallstones and their link to increased cholesterol in older adults? Has this ailment affected you or a loved one?

_____

6. Reflect on the issue of constipation, which may become more common with age. How have you adapted your lifestyle or sought medical guidance to address this concern?

_____

_____

_____

_____

_____

7. In the context of pill esophagitis, consider the practices you've adopted for taking medications. How can you ensure safe and effective medication administration?

_____

_____

_____

_____

_____

_____

_____

_____

_____

_____

_____

Life-Changing Exercises

1. Develop a personalized plan for addressing gastrointestinal concerns and maintaining gut health as you age, incorporating diet modifications,

medication management, and activity adjustments. Review this strategy often and make any necessary adjustments.

2. Explore strategies for preventing constipation, such as dietary choices and physical activity. Develop a routine and track its impact on your gut health.

3. Consult with a healthcare provider regarding any gastrointestinal conditions or concerns you may be experiencing and discuss management strategies.

4. Organize discussions or workshops on gut health with peers, friends, or family, sharing insights and practices for maintaining optimal GI function.

5. Create a checklist for safe and effective medication administration, including taking medications with water and maintaining an upright position to prevent pill esophagitis. Review and

share this checklist with loved ones to promote safe medication use.

Weighing In

Chapter Summary

This chapter delves into the critical role that weight, metabolism, and nutritional needs play in determining longevity, overall health, energy levels, and physical strength as individuals age. It underlines the significance of maintaining an appropriate weight, engaging in regular exercise, and increasing protein intake to support muscle and bone strength, all of which are essential for well-being.

Energy production is influenced by various factors, including calorie intake, food choices, and body composition. Men typically possess a higher percentage of lean body mass, affecting their energy needs. Body Mass Index (BMI) classifications help categorize individuals into groups such as normal weight, overweight, obese, and underweight, providing a framework for understanding weight in relation to health.

The chapter underscores the importance of tailoring nutritional recommendations to age, gender, and physical activity level. Aging often brings about challenges such as weight loss, a decline in appetite, and a reduction in food variety. Anorexia of aging is a significant issue in this context. Approximately 15% of older adults grapple with malnutrition or undernutrition, a condition that can lead to increased morbidity and mortality.

Key Takeaways

1. Weight, metabolism, and nutritional needs have a profound impact on an individual's longevity, health, energy levels, and physical strength as they age.

2. Maintaining an appropriate weight, engaging in regular exercise, and increasing protein intake are

crucial for supporting muscle and bone strength, which are key elements of well-being.

3. Energy production is influenced by factors like calorie consumption, dietary choices, and body composition, with men generally having a higher percentage of lean body mass.

4. Body Mass Index (BMI) classifications provide a means to categorize individuals into different weight groups, offering insights into the relationship between weight and health.

5. Nutritional recommendations should be personalized based on age, gender, and physical activity level. Aging can lead to challenges like weight loss, diminished appetite, and decreased food variety, with anorexia of aging being a significant concern. Malnutrition and undernutrition affect around 15% of older adults, leading to increased health risks.

Self-Reflection Questions

1. How have you observed the impact of your weight, metabolism, and nutritional choices on your energy levels, strength, and overall health as you've aged?

_____

_____

_____

_____

_____

2. Consider your approach to weight management. What strategies have you employed to achieve or maintain an appropriate weight, and how have they influenced your well-being?

_____

_____

_____

_____

3. Reflect on the factors that contribute to energy production in your daily life, including calorie intake, food choices, and body composition. How do these factors affect your vitality and health?

_____

_____

_____

_____

_____

_____

_____

_____

_____

_____

_____

4. Have you assessed your weight through the lens of BMI classifications? What insights have you gained from these classifications, and how have they informed your approach to weight management?

_____

_____

_____

_____

_____

_____

_____

_____

_____

_____

_____

_____

5. Reflect on your nutritional choices and their alignment with your age, gender, and level of physical activity. How have you adjusted your diet to meet your specific needs?

_____

6. Consider any changes in your appetite, food variety, or nutritional intake that you've experienced with age. How have you navigated these challenges?

_____

_____

_____

_____

_____

_____

_____

_____

_____

_____

_____

7. How aware are you of the issue of anorexia of aging and its potential impact on older adults? How can you support yourself and others in addressing this concern?

_____

_____

_____

Life-Changing Exercises

1. Create a personalized nutrition and exercise plan that aligns with your age, gender, and physical activity level. Review this strategy often and make any necessary adjustments.

2. Explore ways to increase protein intake to support muscle and bone strength. Develop a meal plan that incorporates protein-rich foods and monitor its impact on your physical well-being.

3. Conduct a BMI assessment and discuss the results with a healthcare provider to gain insights into your weight and health. Develop a strategy for achieving or maintaining a healthy weight.

4. Organize discussions or workshops on nutrition and exercise with peers, friends, or family, sharing insights and strategies for healthy aging.

5. If you or a loved one is at risk of malnutrition or undernutrition, consult with a healthcare provider to develop a plan for addressing these concerns and promoting overall well-being.

Sex Talk

Chapter Summary

Aging inevitably brings shifts in our sexual desire, openness, and the way we perceive changes in our bodies, attractiveness, and the duration of arousal and orgasm. These changes can stem from various factors, including health conditions, physical limitations, medications, and the evolving dynamics of life itself. Understanding that sexual response evolves with age, the chapter underscores that it's essential to adapt and navigate these changes.

The sexual response cycle is relatively consistent for both men and women, encompassing four key stages: desire, arousal, orgasm, and resolution. What defines a successful sexual experience as we age is highly subjective and depends on individual preferences and comfort levels. Embracing one's evolving body is a critical aspect of sexual well-being in later years.

Open and honest conversations about sexual orientation and gender identity with family, friends, and healthcare providers are vital for finding creative solutions and ensuring a supportive environment. The chapter also highlights the influence of health factors, such as heart health, smoking, cholesterol, high blood pressure, diabetes, and excessive alcohol consumption, on sexual well-being. Maintaining a healthy lifestyle, including regular exercise, may improve erectile function. For individuals facing erectile dysfunction (ED), the approach involves identifying and addressing underlying conditions, such as diabetes and heart disease management, adopting exercise routines, achieving and maintaining a healthy weight, and reducing smoking and alcohol consumption.

Key Takeaways

1. Aging triggers changes in sexual desire, openness, and body perception, which can be influenced by various factors, including health conditions, physical limitations, medications, and personal experiences.

2. Successful sexual experiences in later years are highly individual and depend on one's comfort level and personal preferences.

3. The sexual response cycle, with stages including desire, arousal, orgasm, and resolution, remains relatively consistent for both men and women.

4. Embracing one's changing body is essential for maintaining sexual well-being in older age.

5. Open conversations about sexual orientation and gender identity are essential for creating an inclusive and supportive environment.

6. Health factors, such as heart health, smoking, cholesterol, high blood pressure, diabetes, and excessive alcohol consumption, can significantly impact sexual health.

7. Regular exercise can improve erectile function, and the management of erectile dysfunction (ED) often involves addressing underlying conditions and adopting a healthier lifestyle.

Self-Reflection Questions

1. How has your perspective on sexual desire and openness evolved as you've aged, and what adaptations have you made to your intimate life in response to these changes?

_____

_____

2. Consider your understanding of the sexual response cycle. How have you navigated the stages of desire, arousal, orgasm, and resolution as you've aged?

_____

_____

_____

_____

_____

_____

_____

_____

_____

_____

_____

3. Reflect on your comfort level with your changing body in the context of sexual well-being. How have you embraced your evolving self?

_____

_____

_____

_____

_____

_____

_____

_____

_____

_____

4. Have you engaged in open conversations about sexual orientation and gender identity with family, friends, or healthcare providers? How have these discussions impacted your approach to intimacy?

_____

5. Reflect on the impact of health factors on your sexual well-being, such as heart health, smoking, or diabetes. How have you integrated healthier lifestyle choices into your intimate life?

_____

_____

_____

_____

_____

6. Have you faced issues related to erectile dysfunction (ED), or do you know someone who has? How have you approached addressing these concerns, considering underlying health conditions and lifestyle choices?

_____

_____

_____

7. Consider the concept of a successful sexual experience as you age. How do you define and measure success in this aspect of your life?

_____

_____

_____

_____

Life-Changing Exercises

1. Develop open communication channels with your partner, family, or healthcare provider to discuss intimate matters, including sexual orientation, gender identity, and your evolving sexual well-being.

2. Explore exercise routines that align with your physical abilities and preferences, aiming to enhance your overall health and potentially improve erectile function.

3. Consider dietary adjustments and lifestyle changes, such as smoking cessation and reducing alcohol consumption, to optimize your sexual health.

4. If you or a loved one faces ED, consult with a healthcare provider to identify and address underlying conditions, and discuss strategies for a healthier lifestyle.

5. Create a supportive network of friends or peers with whom you can openly discuss your experiences and insights regarding sexual well-being in later years, fostering a sense of community and understanding.

Part III. Difficult Decisions

Making Difficult Decisions

Chapter Summary

This chapter explores the topic of difficult choices that elderly people and their families must make. It lays a lot of emphasis on the complex interplay of cultural, religious, familial, and personal variables and how these choices are made. The chapter offers the following six insightful suggestions to help you through these difficult times:

1. Being Prepared: Learning about the possibilities and consequences of choices, planning, and thinking through potential outcomes.

2. Honest and Calm Communication: Holding discussions in a calm and thoughtful setting with

loved ones, friends, and healthcare professionals to make sure all viewpoints are taken into account.

3. Including Loved Ones: Acknowledging the value of including friends and family in the decision-making process and using their advice and insights.

4. Being Patient: Realizing that making tough decisions often takes time, thought, and patience to make the best conclusions.

5. Seeking Outside Assistance: Whenever needed, contact experts and community groups to obtain more knowledge and assistance.

6. Prioritizing Personal Values: Stressing the importance of taking into account the particular values and preferences of an older adult, such as relationships with others, independence, quality of life, and health management.

Additional issues covered in this chapter include senior housing alternatives, employing agency services, hiring carers, and identifying appropriate caregivers. When in-home help is not an option, it emphasizes how crucial it is to give the older person's needs and preferences priority and to foster a positive connection between carers and those receiving care.

Key Takeaways

1. Making difficult decisions for older adults is a complex process influenced by cultural, religious, family, and personal factors.

2. Six guiding principles include being prepared, fostering open and calm communication, involving loved ones, practicing patience, seeking external support, and prioritizing personal values.

3. Decision-making should consider an older adult's unique values, encompassing connections, quality of life, independence, and health management.

4. Options for caregiving include finding suitable caregivers, utilizing paid caregiving services, engaging with agency services, and considering senior housing.

5. The well-being and preferences of the older individual should take precedence in decision-making processes, fostering a compassionate and respectful approach.

Self-Reflection Questions

1. Reflect on a time when you or a loved one faced a challenging decision related to aging or caregiving. How did cultural, religious, and personal beliefs influence the decision-making process?

2. Consider the advice provided in the chapter. How have you employed or can you employ these principles when confronting uncertainty and making difficult decisions?

_____

_____

_____

_____

_____

_____

_____

_____

_____

_____

_____

3. Reflect on the significance of open and calm communication when engaging with friends, family, and medical providers. How can these conversations be facilitated to ensure a thoughtful and inclusive decision-making process?

_____

_____

_____

4. Have you had experience involving family and friends in difficult decisions? How did their support and insights contribute to the resolution?

_____

_____

_____

_____

_____

_____

_____

_____

_____

_____

_____

5. Patience is often crucial when navigating challenging decisions. How have you practiced patience in previous decision-making processes, and what were the outcomes?

_____

_____

_____

_____

_____

_____

_____

_____

_____

_____

_____

_____

6. Think about the role of community organizations and professionals in your decision-making experiences. How have these external sources of support been valuable, and how can they be further utilized?

_____

7. Personal values play a pivotal role in decision-making. Reflect on what truly matters to you or an older adult in your life, such as connections, quality of life, independence, or health management.

_____

_____

_____

_____

_____

_____

_____

_____

_____

_____

_____

Life-Changing Exercises

1. Develop a decision-making framework or checklist that incorporates the six guiding principles: being prepared, open and calm communication, involving loved ones, practicing patience, seeking external support, and prioritizing personal values.

2. Engage in open conversations with friends, family, and medical providers to discuss potential challenges or decisions related to aging and caregiving. Ensure that these discussions are conducted in a supportive and understanding environment.

3. Seek external assistance or guidance from community organizations or professionals to gather additional information and support when making difficult decisions.

4. Prioritize personal values by creating a list or vision statement that outlines what is most important to you or the older adult involved in the decision. Use this as a reference point in decision-making.

5. Consider the options for caregiving, whether in-home, utilizing paid services, agency services, or senior housing. Evaluate these choices in the

context of your or your loved one's unique needs and preferences.

To Move or Not to Move

Chapter Summary

The difficult choice of whether to age in place or look for other living arrangements is covered in detail in this chapter. Aging in place, or choosing to stay in one's existing home as one ages, may come with several difficulties and is a very important choice. Home safety becomes a top priority, particularly when the current setting may not be ideal for those with mobility impairments. Daily necessities like having food, paying bills, taking medicine, handling money, and getting about may call for extra help and care.

It is important to emphasize the significance of local support since its lack may result in serious disease or harm. As living conditions change, there may be an increased danger of social isolation. The chapter promotes accepting practical adjustments, such as adjusting to new surroundings, creating new habits, remodeling houses to improve accessibility, and, if needed, thinking about hiring caretakers.

When considering a relocation, several issues come into play, such as cost, senior housing or nursing facility availability, location, and financial resources. The varied requirements of senior citizens are met by a variety of housing alternatives, including continuing care facilities, assisted living, and nursing facility care. The connection between the elderly person and their family plays a crucial part in the decision-making process when it comes to choosing the best housing and care alternatives.

Key Takeaways

1. Aging in place, or remaining in one's current residence as they age, can be challenging due to issues such as home safety and mobility limitations.

2. Daily needs, including food, bill management, medication, finances, and transportation, may require additional assistance as individuals age in place.

3. The presence of local support is crucial, as its absence can lead to health and safety concerns.

4. A risk of social isolation can arise when living circumstances change, emphasizing the importance

of realistic changes and seeking support from caregivers or professionals.

5. When considering a move, various factors, including location, finances, the availability of senior housing or nursing home options, and affordability, influence the decision.

6. Assisted living, nursing home care, and continuing care facilities cater to individuals with different needs and circumstances.

7. The relationship between the older person and their family plays a pivotal role in determining the most suitable care and housing options.

Self-Reflection Questions

1. Reflect on your current living arrangements and your perspective on aging in place. What are the specific challenges or considerations you face, especially in terms of home safety and mobility?

_____

_____

_____

_____

_____

---

2. Consider your daily needs and how they are currently being addressed. Are there areas where you require assistance, and if so, how have you sought support or made necessary adjustments?

---

3. Reflect on the importance of local support in your life. How have you benefited from local resources and community assistance, and how can these be further utilized?

_____

_____

_____

_____

_____

4. Think about the potential for social isolation when living circumstances change. How have you adapted to new environments, routines, or caregiving arrangements to combat this risk?

_____

_____

_____

5. If you're contemplating a move, examine the various factors that influence this decision, including location, financial resources, and housing options. What are the primary considerations guiding your choice?

_____

_____

_____

_____

_____

_____

_____

_____

_____

_____

_____

6. Explore the housing options available, such as assisted living, nursing home care, and continuing care facilities. How do these align with your or your loved one's specific needs and preferences?

_____

_____

_____

_____

7. Reflect on the role of family in decision-making. How has your family's input influenced your choices regarding care and housing, and how have these conversations evolved?

_____

_____

_____

_____

Life-Changing Exercises

1. Conduct a home safety assessment or seek professional assistance to identify and address potential safety hazards in your current living environment.

2. Create a comprehensive checklist that outlines your daily needs and the areas where assistance or support is necessary. Use this checklist as a reference for seeking the appropriate help and making necessary adjustments.

3. Establish connections with local support services and organizations that can provide assistance with daily needs or home safety enhancements. Ensure that your list of accessible resources is kept current.

4. If you are considering a move, develop a decision-making matrix that incorporates key factors like location, financial resources, and housing options. Use this matrix to systematically evaluate your choices.

5. Engage in open and considerate discussions with family members or loved ones to explore various care and housing options, taking into account the unique needs and preferences of the older individual.

Do I Need to Stop Driving?

Chapter Summary

The chapter addresses how aging-related physical, visual, and cognitive impairments are contributing to an increase in older adult fatal accidents and deaths per mile driven. It highlights the need to work with medical professionals to maximize an older adult's driving prowess and the necessity of driving evaluations or consultations with healthcare professionals. The advantages of more recent cars with accident avoidance systems and individualized adaptations are also highlighted in this chapter.

Through driving simulation and on-road examinations, professionals in driving rehabilitation may provide crucial help. It lists warning indications of possible driving issues, including but not limited to honking at other vehicles, collisions, becoming lost, being easily distracted, interacting with law enforcement, having trouble rotating the head while reversing, running into curbs, becoming agitated, and not seeing traffic signals. The chapter recommends taking into account practical options for older individuals to go about, including walking, taxis, public transit, hospital shuttles, mini-cars, volunteer driver programs, and for-profit, private elder care services.

Key Takeaways

1. Increasing rates of fatal accidents and fatalities per mile driven among older adults highlight the importance of assessing driving capabilities.

2. Various medical conditions can affect safe driving, and older adults should collaborate with medical providers to optimize their abilities.

3. Consulting healthcare providers or undergoing a driving assessment can enhance the safety of an older adult's driving.

4. The introduction of newer cars equipped with crash avoidance technologies holds promise for reducing accidents.

5. Modifying vehicles to suit individual needs can enhance driving abilities.

6. Driving rehabilitation specialists can provide valuable support through driving simulation and on-road evaluations.

7. Indications of potential driving problems include specific behaviors and experiences that should prompt a reevaluation of driving abilities.

8. Realistic transportation alternatives for older adults encompass walking, public transportation, taxi services, community transportation, hospital shuttles, mini-cars, volunteer driver programs, and private for-profit senior care services.

Self-Reflection Questions

1. Reflect on your or a loved one's current driving capabilities. Have you noticed any changes or difficulties while driving due to physical, visual, or cognitive factors associated with aging?

_____

_____

_____

_____

_____

_____

_____

_____

_____

_____

_____

2. Consider the medical conditions mentioned in the chapter, such as cataracts or diabetes. Have any of these conditions impacted your driving safety, and if so, have you consulted with a healthcare provider for guidance?

_____

_____

_____

3. Reflect on your openness to undergoing a driving assessment or encouraging a loved one to do so. How do you approach the idea of assessing and potentially improving driving capabilities?

_____

_____

_____

_____

_____

_____

_____

_____

_____

_____

_____

4. Explore the concept of newer vehicles with advanced safety features. Have you considered upgrading to a car equipped with crash avoidance technologies to enhance safety on the road?

_____

_____

_____

_____

_____

_____

_____

_____

_____

_____

_____

_____

5. Think about the potential modifications that can be made to your current vehicle to better accommodate your needs as an older driver. What adjustments could improve your driving experience?

_____

6. If you or a loved one has encountered driving challenges, consider the possibility of consulting a driving rehabilitation specialist. How open are you to this form of support, and what expectations do you have?

_____

_____

_____

_____

_____

_____

_____

_____

_____

_____

_____

_____

7. Review the list of potential driving problems outlined in the chapter. Have you experienced any of these indicators, and if so, how have you responded or adapted?

_____

_____

Life-Changing Exercises

1. Engage in open and considerate conversations with healthcare providers to assess your or your loved one's driving capabilities. Discuss any identified challenges and potential solutions.

2. Explore the possibility of upgrading to a newer vehicle equipped with crash avoidance technologies to enhance safety on the road.

3. Consider potential modifications to your existing vehicle to better accommodate your needs as an older driver. Consult with experts or specialists in this field for guidance.

4. If driving challenges are present, research and connect with driving rehabilitation specialists to explore driving simulation and on-road evaluations.

5. Create a personalized transportation plan that incorporates the realistic alternatives mentioned in

the chapter, taking into account your specific needs and preferences.

Who Will Speak for Me?

Chapter Summary

The significance of appointing a representative to make medical choices on a patient's behalf is emphasized in this chapter, particularly in cases of severe sickness or dementia. Usually specified by a healthcare proxy, this person has the power to make choices on behalf of the patient if the patient is unable to do so. The patient's wishes should be known to the proxy, and a backup proxy should be prepared.

When talking about medical choices, it's important to be open and take the patient's values into account. A health care priority form evaluation and completion are also emphasized in this chapter. If a patient is unable to communicate their wishes, a living will outline the kinds of medical care they would desire. The state may appoint a surrogate to act in a patient's best interests if the patient does not have a chosen proxy.

Key Takeaways

1. Designating a health care proxy is essential to ensure that someone can make medical decisions on your behalf in situations where you cannot express your preferences.

2. The health care proxy should be someone who knows you well and understands your values and care preferences.

3. Consider selecting a backup proxy in your health care proxy document to have a contingency plan in place.

4. Engage in open and detailed conversations with your health care proxy to discuss various medical scenarios, ensuring that your values and preferences are understood.

5. A living will is a crucial document that specifies the types of medical treatments you would want or not want in situations where you cannot communicate your preferences.

6. Regularly review and complete a health care priority form to ensure your medical preferences are up to date.

7. In the absence of a designated proxy, a surrogate designated by the state can make medical decisions in your best interests.

Self-Reflection Questions

1. Reflect on the process of designating a health care proxy. How can you identify someone who knows you well and can represent your values and care preferences effectively?

2. Consider the scenarios you would like your health care proxy to address when making medical decisions on your behalf. How will you communicate your values and preferences effectively to them?

_____

_____

_____

_____

_____

3. Reflect on the importance of a living will. What specific medical treatments or interventions are essential for you to address in this document to ensure your wishes are respected?

_____

_____

_____

4. Explore the process of discussing medical decisions with your health care proxy. How can you engage in open and comprehensive conversations to ensure they understand your values and preferences?

_____

_____

_____

_____

5. Review the concept of a health care priority form. How can you ensure that this document remains up to date and accurately reflects your medical preferences?

_____

_____

_____

_____

6. Imagine a scenario in which you are unable to make a medical decision, and you do not have a designated proxy. How would you feel about the state designating a surrogate to make decisions on your behalf?

_____

_____

_____

_____

_____

_____

_____

_____

_____

_____

_____

7. Reflect on the role of these documents in preserving your autonomy and ensuring that your medical decisions align with your values and preferences.

_____

_____

_____

_____

_____

_____

_____

_____

_____

_____

_____

_____

Life-Changing Exercises

1. Initiate a conversation with a potential health care proxy to discuss your values, care preferences, and the responsibilities associated with this role.

2. Create a living will that outlines your specific preferences regarding medical treatments and interventions. Share this document with your health care proxy and ensure it is accessible when needed.

3. Review and update your health care priority form regularly to reflect any changes in your medical preferences or priorities.

4. Familiarize yourself with state regulations and provisions for surrogate designations in case you do not have a designated proxy. Understand the implications of this scenario and consider designating a proxy if you haven't already.

5. Encourage friends and loved ones to complete their own health care proxy and living will documents, fostering open discussions about

medical preferences and care priorities within your social circle.

Self-Evaluation Questions

1. Have you effectively summarized and understood the key concepts and takeaways from each chapter in the workbook?

_____

_____

_____

_____

_____

_____

_____

_____

_____

_____

2. Have you successfully applied the self-reflection questions and life-changing exercises to your personal understanding and experiences throughout the workbook?

_____

_____

_____

_____

3. How confident are you in your ability to make informed and thoughtful decisions related to aging, health, and caregiving after completing this workbook?

_____

_____

_____

_____

_____

_____

_____

_____

_____

_____

_____

4. Have you identified specific areas in your life where you can implement changes or improvements based on the insights gained from the workbook?

_____

_____

_____

_____

_____

_____

_____

_____

_____

_____

_____

5. How well have you grasped the importance of open communication and support when making decisions related to aging, health, and caregiving?

_____

6. Have you explored and understood the significance of legal documents such as health care proxies and living wills in planning for your future care and medical decisions?

_____

_____

_____

_____

_____

_____

_____

_____

_____

_____

_____

7. To what extent have you considered the role of cultural, religious, and personal beliefs in the decisions you make regarding aging and health?

_____

_____

_____

_____

8. How prepared do you feel to engage in discussions with healthcare providers, caregivers, and loved ones regarding your future care preferences and priorities?

_____

_____

_____

_____

_____

_____

_____

_____

_____

_____

_____

9. Have you developed a deeper appreciation for the importance of home safety and accessibility as you age?

_____

_____

_____

_____

_____

_____

_____

_____

_____

_____

_____

10. How well do you understand the various housing and care options available for older adults, and are you prepared to make informed decisions in this regard?

_____

11. In what ways have you enhanced your ability to provide support and assistance to older adults in your life, whether family members or friends?

_____

_____

_____

_____

12. How confident are you in your understanding of the challenges and changes associated with aging, and how they affect daily living and medical decisions?

_____

_____

_____

_____

13. Have you recognized the significance of maintaining a balance between the quantity and quality of life as you age, and are you prepared to make adjustments to achieve this balance?

_____

_____

_____

_____

14. To what degree have you internalized the need for self-awareness and self-advocacy when making decisions about your own health and care as you age?

_____

_____

_____

_____

_____

15. Have you taken the lessons learned from this workbook and applied them to foster better communication, understanding, and support within your social and family networks when addressing aging and health-related concerns?

_____

_____

_____

_____

_____

_____

_____

Made in the USA
Monee, IL
23 April 2024

57397714R00184